Sliver of the Moon

Concetta Tina Scarpitti

authorHOUSE®

AuthorHouse™
1663 Liberty Drive
Bloomington, IN 47403
www.authorhouse.com
Phone: 1 (800) 839-8640

Published by AuthorHouse   12/08/2016

ISBN: 978-1-5246-5289-0 (sc)
ISBN: 978-1-5246-5288-3 (e)

Print information available on the last page.

A Walk on The Water

He steps onto the ashen rocks to escape
Ever so faintly, he tiptoes over the waves of the landscape,
He manages to keep his breath above sea level
He meets the creature on the other side, the devil.
Eyes peer and sear through his heart
He recovers quickly and sets his battle apart,
Taking it to another level
He becomes the creature, the devil
The evil lurks into her soul walking on the water
It gets magenta-red and gets even hotter,
Suddenly it has met its' Fate
It succumbs to nothing but slate.

Concetta Tina Scarpitti

Aisles of Lavender

Purplish flowers bloom on site
Feel good inside and its` day meets night,
Meadows at your door, no longer air-tight
Above the clouds, nature is but a sight.
Scent of nirvana breathing new air
Beauty at your fingertips, skin so fair,
Empowering thoughts of wisdom to share
Musky oil, her eyes are in a deep, intrusive stare.
Lips so reluctant to kiss him good-night
Shivers in the wind suddenly shift right,
The ocean meets the sky quite contrite
Aisles of lavender meet the meadow at midnight.

Concetta Tina Scarpitti

All of Your Strength

She strives to regain her strength
To move forward, she lacks breath,
Unable to generate another word
She is unaware what has occurred.
Losing the movement in her body so fragile
She is now in tremendous denial,
She is slowly losing her mobility
And becoming more desperate by agility.
Surpassing all that she lived for
She no longer has an open door,
Strength collapses by her fears
And she is convinced she doesn't have a year.
She strives to regain her strength
To move forward she lacks breath,
Unable to generate another word
She is unaware what has occurred.

Concetta Tina Scarpitti

An Angel With a Beating Heart

Flutter your fuschia wings, my angel of wisdom
Spread the glorious love to your kingdom,
Open your heart mesmerized by the purity of gold
Allow the pain to slip away, let the story unfold.
Shower your speckles of treasures from above
And splash my face with unconditional love,
Make those who don`t know you believe in the miracle
Allow your silhouette to be the graceful spectacle.
Your love overpowers all hearts in harmony
You were always a blessing, even through a tragedy,
You are forever my angel who keeps my heart beating
Who takes away my fears, and release the empowering.

Concetta Tina Scarpitti

Beyond Memories

She is asleep and sees your silhouette
She places her sense of touch at her fingertips,
An arson fire has been pre-set
Memory after memory, leaving an imprint.
Shaken by a virtual reality
She awakens, although her eyelashes don't open so freely,
I don't know if she is living a dream
Or if this indeed is her purgatory.
Although she cannot get her eyes to open so easily
She feels a sudden peace of tranquility,
As if she is going to appear suddenly
She is truly blinded by your memory.

Concetta Tina Scarpitti

Bleeding Rose

Thorns prick her finger of innocence
Breaking veins, bleeding soul of her evanescence,
She spills her broken heart
And now becomes the woman she was taught.
Be strong, firm and believe
You can do anything in this life of deceit,
Be true to yourself even if you have to bite your lip
And listen to your heart, even if at times it might dip,
Look in the mirror, innocence fades
She cuts like a knife with her own razor blade.
A bleeding rose spills onto her fingerprint
She rises amongst the ashes filled with bitter mist.

Concetta Tina Scarpitti

Blindness

Twitching in your burning eyes, stinging from behind the retina
So painful, you fall to your knees with no stamina,
Trying to allow yourself to stand tall
Pitter, patter, your eyes aglow, remain listening to the endless rainfall.
Every drop, erasing the next one ever so lightly
Dragging your heels in knee-deep,
Teeth gritting lips bleed so slightly
You begin to drown in your eyes as you sleep.
You are standing in an eclipse with a dark shadow of glory
When should you be telling your story?
The truth which lies through the ripple of the waves
What you cannot reverse will remain unscathed.

Concetta Tina Scarpitti

Broken Arrows

Hope breaks her fortunes so grown
Faith awaits her love forlorn,
Trust erupts her heart of stone
Praying for higher dreams of her own.
Setting aside her needs, her story
Opening her arms of sweet glory,
Her platform sits before her throne
Awaiting her Fate, she reaches her dome.
Defined by odds, she wins gold
She finds her soul, let the truth be told,
And falls down the path so narrow
She's been hit by a broken arrow.

Concetta Tina Scarpitti

Broken Wings

---✦---

He curls his long-fingered toes around his needle tree
He caws over his prey and proceeds,
Snatching a ripple of flesh, he dives
This is his only chance to survive.
Unbeckoning calls, he continues his hunt, he stalls
Unwittingly trembling, shivering overall,
It is a chilly night, but very calm indeed
Swinging over his dark shadow of greed.
A prayer is interrupted by the coyotes ahead
Survival is to blame for what's been said,
A neverending success story unless you revive
A lasting moment of being dead or alive.

Concetta Tina Scarpitti

Change

—————✦—————

When all around is adapting to change
It's time for us to breakaway from disturbing chains,
When all else fails, you start again
It's time to save the train from its' derail.
Capture the essence of time standing still
Behind the clouds, lies the window opportunity of will,
In your tender grasp, the future lies ahead
You can't take your words back from what was once said.
Don't take for granted any gifts you receive
Instead, accept what you can get and you shall believe,
In your inner soul, as you trust only thee
And remember to sow what you keep.
Take the beauty into the palm of your hand
Do not sink into ambiguous quick sand,
Live life to the fullest, and turn every page
And you will survive this inevitable world of change.

Concetta Tina Scarpitti

Crystal Waters

Clear, purity of your enveloping soul
Warm embrace, awash consoled,
Established in its` almighty land
Along the seashore lies the endless sand.
Crystallized patterns lap the miles of shore
Overlapped by the angelic waters` downpour,
Tears fade behind the distinct waves of water
As the sunrays breathe internally, they get warmer.
Sifting the sands of the shore
Opening the heart of the oceans` door,
The crystal waters appear
Refreshing start is veneered.

Concetta Tina Scarpitti

Earth Never Saw the Light

When the trees shrink down to their roots
When the flowers separate from their groups,
When the sea departs from the deepest waters
When the burning sun is no longer hotter.
When the clouds step down from the endless sky
When the message is misread and inevitably lie,
When the earth becomes the moonlight
When the stars stop sparkling from so very high.
When the rainstorm rises up, not down
When the world is said to be flat, not round,
When the soul never leaves your body in every way
When the earth never sees the light, until the very next day.

Concetta Tina Scarpitti

Eclipse of the Heart

Partial sunrise, rays of beauty
Shine on her silken face of ingenuity,
The snow queen has stood over my shoulder
Her power struggles are enforced, like a boulder.
Divided hearts, a two-direction road
Whole-hearted, may the truth be foretold,
New feelings, emotions and renewed vows
Desired pieces of hope, broken mirror allowed.
Split roads laid asunder
Completely immersed down under,
Deep below the sea of love
A tidal wave drowns the mirage above.

Concetta Tina Scarpitti

Eyes of Gold

She is a silhouette of purity
She is an experienced woman of maturity,
She is the golden goose who lays her eggs
She is forthcoming in her coming of days.
A heart of gold,
Not young, not old,
A grain of salt, nor bitter
Her heart goes pitter patter.
Eyes of gold ajar
Shone across the room afar,
Incapable of evil
She is inconceivable.
Her power, her majesty role
Something beyond her control,
Fate has questioned her inner strength
She surpasses her successor in bouts of extreme lengths.

Concetta Tina Scarpitti

Eyes of Steel

A heart so full of strength, he pulls all his weight
Pounding heartbeats, never taking a break,
Disguising his voice as he speaks, he awakes
Eyes of steel, he glows through his wisdom, his Fate.

Roads apart, which path to take
Left or right, is it truly Fate,
Painstakingly suffering, she hesitates
Eyes of steel draw on his strength at a speedy rate.

As we once were standing next to one another
We overcome the evil that possesses the weather,
Galvanized paths destructed by broken homes
Eyes of steel pierce through the heart of stone.

Concetta Tina Scarpitti

Face To Face

---◆---

The spoken word has been foretold
You now carry the purity in the centre of a hearts` gold,
The core is what remains with you to hold
As you disappear, a chill of a mighty cold.
As I shiver in mere silence from my Love
The soft music is still playing up above,
Your memory stands still in a time of renaissance
As you take me up to the highest distance.
We feed the birds of an ivory white
We guide each other, a flock blinded by night,
Holding my golden heart, we release our doves
Never letting go until we arrive to the path of Love.
Together we form one direction
Your guidance illuminates our section,
As I stand in your place
We see each other for the second time face to face.

Concetta Tina Scarpitti

Faith

When all else seems surreal
It may be difficult to completely heal,
I pray strongly before the altar of faith
Hands clamping together, I layeth.
We think why these things can be
We ask ourselves the questions before we believe,
Unknowingly doubting the Higher faith
As we absorb ourselves with leftover strength.
We try so much harder to be a purer man
But it doesn't defeat the grasp of His hand,
We can only take the pain to withstand
Every window we open, as He takes an upper hand.

Concetta Tina Scarpitti

Fallen Tree...

As I gaze up to the sparkling stars above your tree
I hear your voice whisper to me,
As you reach out to hold my mighty hand
I see your footprints in the sinking sand.
As I gaze up to the trickling stars above your tree
I feel your mellow, but beating heartbeat,
As you gaze into my glazed eyes,
I am so blinded by the powerful light.
As I gaze up to the illuminating stars above your tree
I pray for only thee,
As I close my restless eyes
I kneel before the burning sunrise.
As I gaze up to the neverending stars above your tree
I awake from my nightmare, which is now reality,
I blow you a kiss goodnight and weep
As I watch over you, as you fall asleep.

Concetta Tina Scarpitti

Father and Daughter

---※---

It is I that aches for you to get well
It is I that wipes away your endless tears,
It is I that held your hand when it swelled
It is I that protected you from your greatest fears.

It is I that let you borrow my shoulder to cry on
It is I that created the road for you to walk along,
It is I that carried you when He snatched you so soon
It is I that showed you the burning sunrise until noon.

It is I that kneels before the road you paved
It is I that sifts the sand of footsteps wave after wave,
It is now that He stands
He will take you to the forever Promised Land.
"Dad(Big Guy) ripose in pace."

Concetta Tina Scarpitti (zingara)

Garnet Petals

---✦---

A blooming, garnet-stone petal curls
Renewing its` past with a fresh new day,
I await for every corner to unfurl
Until it has blown completely away.
I blow every crisp petal of garnet red
I squish its` juices and get it all fingerprinted,
It seems to bleed out, dead
I make room for regrowth and dig at its` foot imprint.
Crackling sequence of red fire
I await the dew to waiver its` past growth,
Raindrops put out the fire with no desire
And eats away at its` youth.

Concetta Tina Scarpitti

Hand In Hand

One last note before you disappear
One last whisper into your ear,
One last attempt to revive your heart
One last prayer before your journey departs.
One last smile before my very own
One last kiss, you'll never feel alone,
One last step, our footprints melt into the sand
One last journey, we walk hand in hand.
One last look before I say good-bye
One last breath before you cry,
One neverending teardrop on your royal crown
One last picture on your breast as you fall down.
One last story between father and daughter
One last story from sad to laughter,
One last wave before you say goodbye
One last stop before we complete our journey.

Concetta Tina Scarpitti

Heart of Darkness

His eyes so surreal and peering
Glued to her sight persevering,
He kneels before her to take her hand
He cannot speak, he sinks deep into the sand.

Emotional cry of his last word
Escaping the maze of a strange world,
He stops abruptly, gasping for breath
She takes his hand, he is seconds from death.

Her eyes meet his steel-blue
Her eyelashes fall down as does the dew,
Sweet gumdrops, she has captured his heart
He will never escape now nor part.

Concetta Tina Scarpitti

Heart of Stone

Sinking deep when it feels down
Holding thoughts pound after pound,
Pain and suffering built inside
Taking life in stride after stride.
Solid-stone, flesh-like skin
Taking the pain deep within,
Not knowing exactly what life holds
Only the tears remain in the eyes blindfold.
Observing nothing but darkness around
Chamber after chamber only surround,
Lost in the odds, all alone
Chased by the human heart of stone.
Tears fall softly, forever they weep
Rushing rivers flow softly in the waters of deep,
Shivers in the bitter, cold wind erupt her scorn
Open arms do dwell upon her welcoming throne.

Concetta Tina Scarpitti

Heart on Fire

Burning sensation, holding onto miracles
Gripping to endless rope,
Surpassing even the most complicated obstacles
Uncertain of a destined hope.
Worthy to strive for the strength He gives her
Faith prevails in her empty hand.
A sight for sore eyes, burning her inner purity
Sins absolve, He stands before the land.
Her heart is on fire
Mayhem and love don't go hand in hand,
Although what doesn't fail is desire
It disappears like the depth of a grain of quicksand.

Concetta Tina Scarpitti

I Am...

Lord, help me to think positively
Lord, tell me I'm beautiful emotionally,
Lord, help me be purely good
Lord, help me be understood.
Lord, I am who I am today
Lord, you are my powerful sunray,
Lord, I am who you've made me to be
Lord, you are my source of energy.
Lord, take away all of my fears
Lord, remove my sins until I see clearly,
Lord, take away all the painful layers beneath
Lord, remove the negativity.
Lord, carry my strength to higher ground
Lord, pray for all who haven't yet found,
Lord, carry my soul, I do confide
Lord, pray for all, my journey alongside.

Concetta Tina Scarpitti

I am in Flight

Birds on a wire scatter above
Swooning in a complete circle of love,
A heart of gold is what they create
I know now that this is your creation to my Fate.
You're giving me a message of truth
In kindrid coded hearts, an unknown sleuth,
Petals of stone, no stone overturned
May the silhouette be seen, I have yearned.
One message is a token of hope to lead me to you
Opening my eyes to the number one truth,
Waves on the water, filling their thirst
I always put not myself, but you first.
Birds in –flight flock as a team
Creating a paradise for your return,
In-flight, they await their master of freedom
And join the world to view their unison as one.

Concetta Tina Scarpitti

Immortals

Dismal mountains in the forbidden outback
Colossal peaks score each sharp edge above,
Wolves prepare themselves and the pack
The vultures tear into the imaginary doves.
Dark worlds meet in the middle of the circle
Opening the gallows so deep between the crevice,
Beating the odds between black and purple
Secreting the sins, he begins his penance.
Masks unveil the absolute truth
Disguises reveal their true identity,
The elderly introduce the youth
The mirage is forbidden to communicate with its' entity.

Concetta Tina Scarpitti

In Time

One step forward, one step behind
When will we ever be able to find,
What we have been searching for so very long
Maybe we'll find the answers at the end of the song.
I capture all reasonings
I capture all destinies,
We seize to search for the ultimate truth
Lying beneath the surface of today's youth.
Until science gives us the answers to find
We may now be in a bind,
One step forward, one step behind
When will we ever be able to find the time?

Concetta Tina Scarpitti

Love

---◆---

She moved through the distance ahead
Gazing the mist where the children weep,
Sifting through sands of the mead'
Peering through ponderous waters too deep.
Chirping sounds created up afar
Movement withholds the action in place,
Seeking the darkened memories within a star
Two unknown worlds bound to be traced.
Fleeing odds and spaces of hollow
A hearts' chamber can only survive bloodflows,
Tightening thoughts, decayed to be swallowed
Circulating smoothly, enough to destroy.
Nature relieved its' suffering pain
Willows sway over the thick mist,
Tender waters prepared their ordain
Warm thoughts, forever are missed.

Concetta Tina Scarpitti

Midnight Hue

The crisp, auburn red sun is burning my face
You give me a new breath in every trace,
Your footsteps remain in the sifty sands
You reach out for my praying hands.
You show me you are in a peaceful place
You mark every footprint with every pace,
You whisper my name with the greatest Love
You then disappear up and above.
Thank-you for letting me see your spiritual face
Thank-you for ensuring me your secure place,
Thank-you for warming my cupped hands in disguise
Thank-you for drying my tears from my eyes.

Concetta Tina Scarpitti

Mildew Drops

The rain splashes over her face
Renewing her existing place,
Extracting her footsteps, do retrace
Refreshing dew drops, petals of lace.
The rain pours down its' almighty plea
Encircling, crystal drops fall, one, two, three,
Puddles deepen, their strength open their arms so freely
Entangling her in the dew tree branches so strongly.
Precipitation washes her eyes
Her feelings and gestures are in disguise,
Mildness turns to a sun that rises
She breathes in the warm air of dryness.

Concetta Tina Scarpitti

My Wings of Gold

She spreads her fiery wings of bold
Fire erupts, cinching the charcoal,
She awakens the spirits of the God
Illuminating her wings of pure gold.
Eyes of purity set agaze so solid
Hands fold together to uphold,
Hearts of wisdom enhance her warmth, not cold
Illuminating her wings of pure gold.
Mercy graces in the hands so forlorn
Shoulders unveiled, a perch of a raven sold,
Counting the many who flock twofold
Illuminating her wings of pure gold.
Time is of the essence which cannot be put on hold
Minutes turn to hours until she is reborn,
She walks with her head high to her throne
Illuminating her wings of pure gold.

Concetta Tina Scarpitti

Raven

Spread out like the Goddess of Love
Escaping sin, he enters the gallows of stone,
He puts forth his blackened dove
He settles into his niche, a graphite throne.

Tilting his crooked neck on an angle
He allows his curiosity to get the better of him,
He paces before the trap setup of mangle
He doesn't respond to goodness, only sin.

He is trapped before the darkness settles in
He agrees to be good if you let him go,
He knows he's lost, doesn't surrender, does not win
He is the only splattered mark on the icy cold blanket of snow.

Concetta Tina Scarpitti

Shadow Beside Her

Her outline of her cookie cutter life to be
Her outlook on life becomes her destiny,
Her pursuit of happiness is what she foresees
A silhouette of her beauty so effortlessly.

She has a sparkle to her when she appears
Her glowing skin of blush is seared,
Her sweet heart pours her greatest deeds
She stands before her throne of veneer.

Splashes of glass spill from her eyes
Tears of joy stand still in disguise,
She sees her shadow standing beside
Only to conclude she has passed to the other side.

Concetta Tina Scarpitti

She is Gone

One moment, she appeared
One moment, she flutters toward me,
One moment, she disappears
One moment, she has me believe.
One minute to speak one word
One minute to hug her and love unconditionally,
One minute to move forward
One minute to reveal a word after breathing.
One hour to lift her spirit
One hour to fold her hands to pray,
One hour to change this poem to lyrics
One hour to physically walk away.
One day to depart and take her journey
One day to change her hearts' destiny,
One day to relay her secrets of deceit
One day to exist, one year to be truly free.
One moment to play your cards on the table
One moment to interact like no tomorrow,
One moment to change from folk to fable
One moment to lift her happy eyes to sorrow.

Concetta Tina Scarpitti

Shoreline

Time expires as the years go by
The waters overlap nature's shoreline,
Days turn to restless nights
The sky meets the endless sunrise.
Clear, blue waters of a fallen cascade
Deep oceans, sharp-tide blades,
Overturn the strength of its' tides
The rocks kiss nature's waters so very high.
The sun burns the waters of deep
The shadows of footsteps lie on sands so steep,
The air is crisp, as a blanket of linen
The sheets of sand lie next to the sun made to glisten.
The beach kisses the shoreline
The stars twinkle the sky line of tiger's eye,
The sea has hues of emerald green so very fine
Hear the sand kiss the shoreline in overtime.

Concetta Tina Scarpitti

Silhouette of Your Face

The iridescent rainbow splashes over the mountain ice-glacier scene
The rain feeds its' thirst on the frozen rocks so surreal,
The mountain top kisses the illuminating sun so clearly
The unbearable heat is burning like melted steel.
The acoustic voices erupt in the crisp crust between the earth
The overlapping waves kiss the sea against the rocks I appeal,
The hues combine and form a rainbow of mirth
The tide is moving in, so serene.
The ice caps volcanically erupt and wake up the pillars
The reproduction of natures' place,
The moonlight glowing overpowers the stars
Your silhouette appears, the silhouette of your untouchable face.

Concetta Tina Scarpitti

Sliver of the Moon

---*---

Discovering doubts of reality faced
Reality was not a disguise,
Thinking of smiles blended with disgrace
Soft, mellow sounds of nature's cries.

She gazed down below and peered up above
Clutching hands, praying before spiritual shadows,
Surviving the helpless, needing to feel loved
Within the distance remain unopened gallows.

She spreads her wings to send all her love
She moves through life with power of need,
Opening her heart to natures' doves
Giving her message, love, pouring her great deed.

Concetta Tina Scarpitti

Snow Queen

She stands before her throne
Grounded by the rugged rocks and impurities of pebblestone,
Each thumbprint raises a story to tell
Awaiting the punchline she says so well.

Her laughter highlights her personality
She is envied by girls living outside her reality,
A characteristic surrounded by joy and wisdom
She walks down the aisle, her kingdom.

What is her name?
She is your mother, sister, daughter and one in the same,
A beauty of purity, she arises so serene
She is the well-known daughter of the Snow Queen.

Concetta Tina Scarpitti

Sometimes

When the earth showers us with porous rain
Sometimes it washes away only part of the strain,
But not necessarily erasing the heavy pain
Only pellets of gold could solidify its' ordain.

Living outside substance, your heart is put aside
Sometimes playing Jekyll, sometimes Mr. Hyde,
One speckle on a cobblestone is chipped a bit
And all of earth can crumble in under a minute.

Laughing hysterically, crying the next
Sometimes makes her wonder about your vortex,
Ambiguous of her emotions of love and hate
A lesson she doesn't wish to foretell her own Fate.

Sometimes not able to keep a promise so unique
Fallen into a hole so very deep,
Sometimes it is what it doesn't seem to be
And people are indecisive in their conspiracy.

Concetta Tina Scarpitti

Stitched Lips

*Your words are sitting alone on the throne
It is not a belief I do condone,
I am uncertain of spoken words from generous lips I trace
As thy arms embrace at a slower pace.*

*Escaping from a runaway place
Releasing the chains of a broken space,
Surrounded by negative energy of defeat
Pretending the untouched is secure and neat.*

*Deadly markings still sit on the grounds
Spooled by the activity of dirty, stained hands,
Unexplained tempering unchartered waters
Leave the tears behind, and begin the laughter.*

*Don't take the crime seriously, you're fooling only thine
You're a fool living off a silly head of a dime,
Teach only good things to enrich young minds of rich, not poor
You are but an open revolving door.*

Concetta Tina Scarpitti

Tears of Stone

---⁂---

Trickling down her cheek
Waterdrops fall so deep,
Negative energy binded by intensity
She falls down to her knees.

Unveils her mask of masquerade
She isn't herself, an unknown shade,
She disrobes, a feeling of ambiguity
She joins the forces of uncertainty.

Her fingertips become someone
Unfortunate events lead to none,
True innocence, no ties to freedom
Unknown, but known to some.

Her innocence fades
To a gloomy shade of grey,
Marking her territory, she is alone
Sitting before her, her shadow in stone.

Concetta Tina Scarpitti

Thank-you Father

---✦---

Your eyelashes fall down one by one
You always knew how to teach the words of wisdom,
You made me happy with every shining smile
And reminded me that I was your favourite little girl.
You allowed me to express myself
You taught me how rich life was without wealth,
You pronounced my first spoken word, `Papa`
You teased mom so proudly which ended in laughter.
You made me what I am today
You are my standing ground, my rock, my clay,
You made me feel special when we danced the night away
And welded me a steel flower arch for my perfect wedding day.
You are forever, my dear Father
A kind hearted knight in shining armour,
``Mio bello papa,`` just a token to say thank-you for your guiding hands
I shall raise the dissipated ashes into crystallized sands.
``Papa, grazie per la cresciuta.``
``Dad, thanks for raising me, as I take care of mom as I promised. ``

Concetta Tina Scarpitti

The Lord Hath Spoken

---*---

The Lord gives thine `tis hand
The Lord gathers the seeds of His land,
The Lord awaits your undying Fate
The Lord takes `tis brush and begins to paint.
The Lord has opened up a whole new day
The Lord reads the words to say,
``I pour my adoration over and above``
His wings open with porous Love.
The Lord guides thine own soul
The Lord opens `tis arms to console,
The Lord hath spoken the words of wisdom
The Lord hath given us the Life of reason.

Concetta Tina Scarpitti

There Is...

When there's no heart, there's no feel
When there's no bandaid, there's no heal,
When there's no night, there's no day
When there's no opinion, there's no say.

When there's no silence, there's no words
When there's no fish, there's no lure,
When there's no life, there's no legacy
When there's no hope, there's no peace.

When there's no curve, there's no bend
When there's no road, there's no end,
When there's no voice, there's no speech
When there's no mountains, there's no peak.

When there's no revision, there's no change
When there's no two, there's no exchange,
When there's no sun, there's no light
When there's no moon, there is only night.

Concetta Tina Scarpitti

Unwanted Good-byes

We are at the edge on cliffs' end
Nature rides with nightless cries,
The route has far yet to bend
Realistically saying our unwanted good-byes.

We gaze through a crowded room
Hoping the smiles won't die,
We face the generations' bloom
Realistically saying our unwanted good-byes.

Slipping away from our very hands
Awaiting heart's contempt to lie,
We carry each other, unknown to stand
Realistically saying our unwanted good-byes.

Pain and suffering meant to behold
Eyes do ponder the mid-hours' sky,
Life's but a walking shadow of cold
Realistically saying our unwanted good-byes.

Concetta Tina Scarpitti

Waiting for a Sign

---✦---

Sweet, succulent gumdrops surround your oak tree
Underground of six feet deep,
This is the paradise you chose to be
Where the sunshine illuminates its` seeds.
Angels lurk amongst the silky silhouette
Shadows are overpowering your angel sight,
I think of our first meeting when we met
Now the beauty of day turns to a mighty cold night.
I sit patiently for your whisper
Filling the purity in my emptied heart,
Shivering as the petals are, an aged petal gets crispier
Filling my heart with warmth, a spirit appears in the midnight dark.
Darkness prevails under the clouds of wonder
The moon glows in the midst and winks freely,
I sit awaiting your sign as I ponder
Now I know you have reached me.

Concetta Tina Scarpitti

Waters of Deep

Broken glass scattered amongst the waves
Drowning her sorrows in a shallow grave,
Shadows of dark, cut inside like a knife
Emotions tangled in a web out of sight.

A hidden agenda covers up her true self
An old testament still remains on ones' shelf,
A degree of truth sets her degree
Broken chains, now make her free.

Breathable circumstance of choice
Benefitting the ultimate source,
A dart doesn't centre itself
With no strategy, do you make stealth?

Concetta Tina Scarpitti

You're There, Now You're Here

Good morning, you're standing in the light of love
You appear amongst the scattered flying doves,
You direct the sunlight my very way
You stare into my eyes, yet no words do you say?

Good afternoon, by heart is pulsating beat after beat
You pour the burning light on my tender feet,
By now I am running to your sight
I am falling deep into what is a wind of flight.
Good evening, my whisper is now a loud voice
Hoping you would hear the noise,
I leave behind my echo, and cannot see
And turn to find you standing before me.
Goodnight, I have run into the spirit of love you've set
Your heart, your soul, your silhouette,
In my heart, I carefully touch your spirit so near
Now I see that you were there, now you're here…
in my heart.

Concetta Tina Scarpitti

Printed in the United States
By Bookmasters